Zoo Animals
PHOTOS AND FACTS FOR EVERYONE

BY ISIS GAILLARD

Learn With Facts Series

Book 130

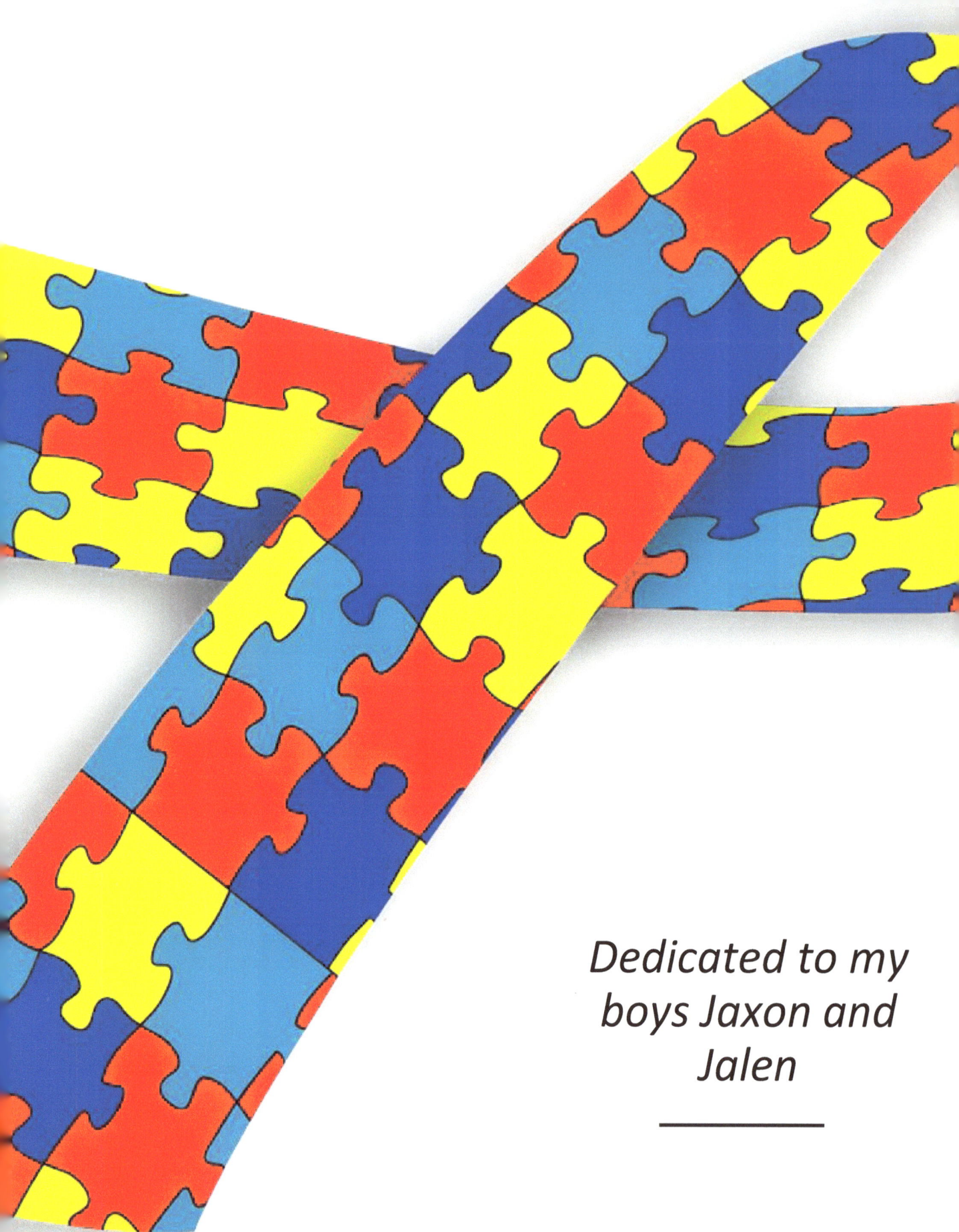

Dedicated to my boys Jaxon and Jalen

_____

CONTENTS

Image Credits: Royalty-free images reproduced under license from various stock image repositories.

Isis Gaillard. Zoo Animals: Photos and Facts for Everyone (Learn With Facts Series Book 130). Ebook Edition. Learn With Facts an imprint of TLM Media LLC

eISBN: 979-8-88700-849-3
ISBN-13: 979-8-88700-147-0

Introduction

Oh my, lions, tigers, and bears! The zoo is home to a wide variety of land animals, including those whose natural habitat, or environment, is the jungle, forest, or desert. The giant panda is one of the most well-liked creatures at the National Zoo in Washington, DC. The panda bear, which has its origins in China, is now one of the most well-known and critically endangered species in the world. Elephants, giraffes, and apes are some big land mammals that are frequently seen in zoos. Zoologists, who research the physical traits and behavior of animals, work to design an area at the zoo that is comparable to the animals' natural habitats.

1. Armadillo

All but one of the 20 different species of armadillo are found in Latin America. The only species whose distribution includes the United States is the well-known nine-banded armadillo.The term "armadillo," which is Spanish for "little armored one," describes the bony plates that most of these peculiar-looking creatures have covering their backs, heads, legs, and tails. Only living mammals with similar shells are armadillos.Armadillos, which are related to anteaters and sloths, often have small eyes and a snout that is pointed or shovel-shaped.

2. Sea Lion

Eared seals include both sea lions and fur seals. They can be distinguished from real seals by their apparent ear flaps. While genuine seals typically utilize their back flippers to swim, they also use their fore flippers to help them move through the water. Although some men have lighter coloration on their head, nose, sides, hind, and belly, males are typically a dark chestnut brown color. Typically, females and young animals are tan. Both sexes have a silky, one-haired coat that also sets them apart from genuine seals. Males grow a visible crest, which runs lengthwise over the top of their skull, at the age of five, giving them a high, domed forehead..

3. Peacock

Peacocks are huge, colorful pheasants (usually blue and green) famed for their iridescent tails. More than 60% of the bird's entire body length is made up of these tail feathers, known as coverts, which have characteristic blue, gold, red, and other colored "eye" markings. The enormous train is employed in wooing displays and mating rituals. It has the ability to be arched into an impressive fan that spans the bird's back and touches the ground on each side. According to legend, females select their mates based on the size, color, and quality of these extravagant feather trains.

4. Tiger

The tiger is the largest wild cat in the world and is easily identified by its reddish-orange coat with dark stripes. The three-foot tail of the huge cat is lengthy. The huge cat often weights 450 pounds, which is equivalent to eight children aged 10 years old. It is three feet tall, has four-inch-long teeth, and claws the length of house keys. The strong predator, capable of taking down game like deer and antelope, typically hunts alone. Tigers do not hunt till it is dark. The tiger runs up to an unwary animal and typically lifts it off its feet using its fangs and claws. Smaller prey is typically killed by the tiger breaking its neck; larger prey is destroyed by the tiger biting its throat.

5. Giraffe

In their first year of life, giraffes develop to a height of about 4 feet (1.2 meters). At birth, a baby giraffe stands approximately 6 feet (1.9 meters) tall and weighs approximately 150 pounds (68 kilograms). During their first year of life, lion attacks claim the lives of numerous young giraffes, known as calves. When a giraffe reaches adulthood, its height may frequently keep predators away. However, when giraffes reach down to drink or relax, they still need to be cautious of lions. In order to ensure that at least one giraffe is constantly alert for incoming predators, giraffes typically drink or rest in shifts.

6. Rhinoceros

Black rhinoceroses tend to approach situations by attacking first and asking questions later. A rhino is likely to charge if it detects the scent of a human or anything else foreign. Because rhinos have poor vision, they occasionally charge things like rocks and trees because they think they pose a threat. However, rhinos have great hearing and smell senses. Sometimes rhinos will fight one another. Black rhinos battle with their larger of the two horns on their noses. They occasionally lose their horns, which are formed of a material resembling that of human fingernails, but they regenerate, or grow back. In addition, female rhinos utilize their horns to shield their young from lions, crocodiles, and hyenas.

7. Alpaca

A type of camelid mammal found in South America is the alpaca (Lama pacos). It is comparable to the llama and frequently misidentified as one. Alpacas frequently, meanwhile, are substantially smaller than llamas. Because they are closely related, the two animals can successfully interbreed. Both species are said to have evolved from their wild cousins, the vicua and guanaco, through domestication. Alpacas come in two varieties: the Huacaya alpaca and the Suri alpaca. Alpacas use nonverbal cues to communicate.

8. Leopard

This particular cat can easily descend a tree without assistance. Because it feels so at ease up there, the leopard frequently chases animals and even carries its kills up into the branches. Strong big cats with ties to lions, tigers, and jaguars include leopards. They reside in northeast Africa, central Asia, India, China, and sub-Saharan Africa. However, many of their populations, particularly those outside of Africa, are in danger.Most leopards may be recognized by their pale coloring and unique dark markings. Because of their resemblance to rose petals, those patches are known as rosettes. As they walk through the grass and trees, these patterns conceal their bodies.

9. Jaguar

The third-biggest cat in the world and the largest of South America's big cats is the jaguar. Typically, their fur is tan or orange with black spots that are shaped like roses and are referred to as "rosettes." Some jaguars appear to lack spots because they are so dark. Jaguars do not shy away from water like many other cats do; in fact, they are excellent swimmers. Fish, turtles, and caimans—small, alligator-like creatures—can all be found as prey in rivers. Jaguars also consume larger creatures including tapirs, peccaries, deer, and capybaras. Sometimes they would climb trees to set up an ambush, murdering their prey with a single devastating bite.

10. Emu

The emu (Dromaius novaehollandiae), a ratite relative of the ostrich, is the second-largest extant bird in terms of height. It is the only surviving member of the genus Dromaius and the largest native bird of Australia, where it is endemic. The majority of mainland Australia is included in the emu's range, but once European settlers arrived in Australia in 1788, the Tasmanian, Kangaroo Island, and King Island subspecies went extinct.Emus are brown, flightless birds with long necks and legs that can grow as tall as 1.9 meters (6.2 feet). Emus can run at 48 km/h (30 mph) when necessary, and they are capable of covering enormous distances while foraging on a variety of plants and insects. However, they have been known to go for weeks without eating.

Interesting Facts

1. Zoos also called zoological gardens or zoological parks are places where wild animals are kept for public display.

2. Most long-established zoos exhibit general collections of animals, but some formed more recently specialize in particular groups — e.g., primates, big cats, tropical birds, or waterfowl. Marine invertebrates, fishes, and marine mammals are often kept in separate establishments known as aquariums.

3. The term "zoological garden" refers to zoology, the study of animals. The term is derived from the Greek ζώον, zoon, 'animal', and the suffix -λογία, –logia, 'study of'. The abbreviation "zoo" was first used of the London Zoological Gardens, which was opened for scientific study in 1828 and to the public in 1847.

THE END

Thanks for reading facts about Zoo Animals. I am a parent of two boys on the autism spectrum. I am always advocating for Autism Spectrum Disorders which part of the proceeds of this book goes to many Non-Profit Autism Organizations. I would love if you would leave a review.

Author Note from Isis Gaillard:

Thanks For Reading! I hope you enjoyed the fact book about Zoo Animals.

Please check out all the Learn With Facts and the Kids Learn With Pictures series available.

Visit www.IsisGaillard.com and www.LearnWithFacts.com to find more books in the Learn With Facts Series

More Books In The Series

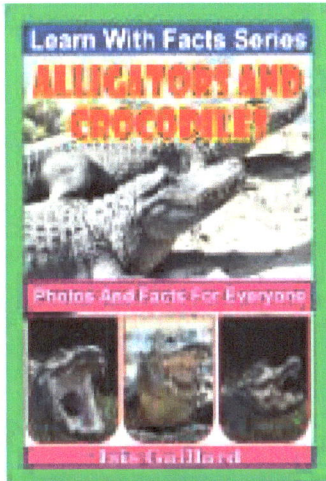

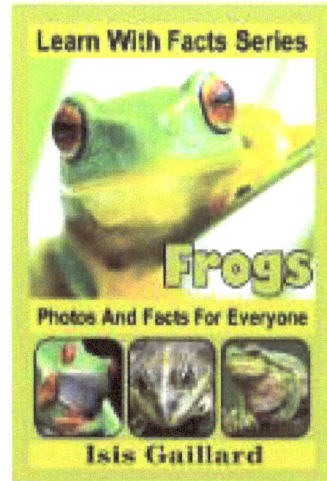

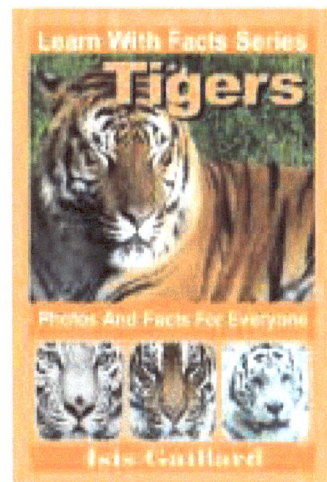

Over 75 books in the Learn With Facts Series.

Set 1

A	L	L	X	R	F	K	Y	S	A	S	I	X	K	P
S	Q	H	Y	N	O	W	O	G	R	B	G	S	O	W
E	L	X	D	B	X	O	B	A	I	A	D	O	R	R
L	G	W	B	Z	E	U	Y	T	L	R	G	F	R	D
E	K	G	O	O	S	B	X	Z	I	A	V	U	U	F
P	L	D	W	H	I	E	H	B	E	I	S	Y	O	S
H	S	D	V	I	C	E	C	T	E	Y	W	C	H	C
A	C	H	I	N	C	H	I	L	L	A	S	A	I	J
N	S	S	B	N	N	F	A	F	J	L	T	Y	A	L
T	O	E	U	T	O	F	P	M	V	E	D	C	I	S
S	O	D	S	M	F	S	V	T	E	R	S	O	W	R
E	R	Z	O	R	A	G	A	H	Y	L	N	Q	V	A
A	A	F	E	L	O	T	C	U	I	S	E	Q	Y	E
G	G	Q	R	G	P	H	O	K	R	A	K	O	L	B
L	N	T	C	X	X	H	Z	P	F	S	E	A	N	B
E	A	L	I	S	E	L	I	D	O	C	O	R	C	S
S	K	D	E	K	V	W	S	N	D	P	N	D	Z	I
S	G	O	H	E	G	D	E	H	S	O	P	F	G	I
F	H	S	R	E	V	A	E	B	P	C	C	I	B	S
A	H	B	P	E	G	I	R	A	F	F	E	S	H	E

Word List

Bears	Dolphins	Kangaroos
Beavers	Eagles	Koalas
Birds	Elephants	Lions
Chameleons	Foxes	Owls
Cheetahs	Frogs	
Chinchillas	Giraffes	
Cougars	Hedgehogs	
Crocodiles	Hippopotamus	
Dinosaurs	Horses	

Set 2

```
Z  G  K  M  V  B  E  E  S  S  O  V  E  E  P
P  E  A  C  O  C  K  S  F  R  A  N  E  Y  H
G  I  P  Z  A  L  L  I  G  A  T  O  R  S  B
C  J  G  A  E  N  F  V  S  U  U  L  Y  C  R
Y  R  R  U  N  L  X  Z  R  G  Q  K  C  S  C
H  S  I  F  A  D  L  Y  E  A  N  O  E  I  K
R  P  C  D  H  N  A  E  G  J  T  I  P  H  S
H  I  F  A  N  W  A  S  I  X  P  O  X  N  S
I  D  Z  A  M  A  P  S  T  P  Q  I  E  A  Y
N  E  F  L  H  E  S  B  U  X  T  T  R  G  H
O  R  L  P  G  M  L  P  T  O  T  B  B  S  S
C  S  A  A  U  M  D  S  A  I  E  A  L  E  I
E  A  M  C  E  N  W  S  K  Z  T  C  R  A  F
R  A  I  A  A  U  N  D  M  S  R  T  W  T  Y
O  L  N  S  S  I  N  K  S  E  F  F  V  U  L
S  J  G  Z  U  A  V  E  N  R  R  T  K  R  L
G  O  O  G  S  O  C  B  A  H  S  I  A  T  E
D  I  N  T  F  C  B  Y  K  Q  Z  C  B  L  J
B  E  A  Q  B  U  T  T  E  R  F  L  I  E  S
P  C  I  N  S  E  C  T  S  E  V  Q  K  S  Z
```

Word List

Alligators	Flamingo	Penguins
Alpacas	Gazelle	Rhinoceros
Bats	Hyena	Sea Turtles
Bees	Iguanas	Snakes
Butterflies	Insects	Spiders
Camels	Jaguars	Tigers
Cats and Kittens	Jellyfish	Zebras
Dogs and Puppies	Pandas	
Fish	Peacocks	

Set 3

```
P  S  G  U  K  P  O  N  I  E  S  C  M  M  S
O  A  N  S  O  C  T  O  P  U  S  E  S  I  E
T  T  R  O  E  R  O  O  S  T  E  R  S  Q  A
C  S  K  R  I  F  K  K  J  M  Y  P  W  S  L
M  Y  J  A  O  P  O  V  J  L  C  I  A  G  S
W  K  C  Q  E  T  R  W  E  S  U  G  N  G  A
H  Z  E  F  I  Y  S  O  R  A  V  S  S  O  N
W  O  L  V  E  S  P  A  C  E  S  A  S  S  D
L  G  Y  Z  W  A  E  S  S  S  Y  N  W  T  S
V  X  T  L  R  B  D  O  N  D  O  D  N  R  E
H  G  I  D  R  R  O  A  Y  G  S  P  S  I  A
W  E  S  A  A  M  C  G  A  T  T  I  E  C  L
U  H  L  Z  X  I  G  R  P  A  A  G  A  H  I
L  O  I  E  L  T  D  E  K  B  R  L  H  E  O
P  L  O  E  X  O  U  R  I  S  F  E  O  S  N
L  N  P  Q  D  A  E  R  D  G  I  T  R  N  S
B  R  P  O  V  E  S  W  T  X  S  S  S  V  S
A  E  M  L  M  L  Y  N  X  L  H  T  E  W  G
D  O  O  X  X  O  W  H  A  L  E  S  S  H  M
K  V  R  A  N  T  E  A  T  E  R  S  A  J  T
```

Word List

Anteater	Parrots	Starfish
Komodo Dragons	Pelicans	Swans
Leopards	Pigs and Piglets	Turtles
Lizards	Polar Bears	Whales
Lynx	Ponies	Wolves
Meerkat	Roosters	
Moose	Scorpions	
Octopuses	Seahorses	
Ostriches	Seals and Sea Lions	

Set 4

```
Z  P  O  R  C  U  P  I  N  E  S  C  M  F  Z
P  K  N  S  K  C  E  O  Y  U  H  A  O  A  I
E  C  H  I  D  N  A  R  F  M  O  E  U  A  H
K  H  C  K  W  Q  E  E  S  E  R  R  N  K  F
R  M  P  L  S  E  U  K  Y  G  O  A  T  S  X
N  A  R  L  D  Q  R  J  N  E  C  H  A  P  V
S  H  C  N  A  O  U  U  G  B  H  P  I  B  L
T  Y  I  C  T  T  P  I  U  B  I  L  N  B  I
C  E  E  S  O  F  Y  F  R  E  C  T  L  Z  V
R  O  G  K  E  O  F  P  Z  R  K  D  I  S  E
F  D  W  I  N  A  N  L  U  R  E  O  O  L  D
E  W  I  S  L  O  G  S  L  N  L  N  O  N
R  E  T  O  V  V  D  X  U  A  S  G  S  T  A
R  C  H  I  P  M  U  N  K  S  M  W  W  H  I
E  W  S  H  A  R  K  S  D  Q  S  A  M  S  N
T  I  D  Y  C  Z  O  O  T  H  O  R  A  D  A
S  Y  T  E  G  U  I  N  E  A  P  I  G  S  M
J  S  E  T  E  S  E  E  R  D  L  O  J  T  S
J  K  H  H  F  R  P  S  K  U  N  K  S  N  A
X  A  R  M  A  D  I  L  L  O  C  E  R  L  T
```

Word List

Armadillo
Buffalo
Chickens
Chipmunks
Cows
Deer
Donkeys
Echidna
Emu

Ferrets
Goats
Guinea Pigs
Llama
Mountain Lions
Platypus
Porcupines
Raccoons
Reindeer

Sharks
Sheep
Skunks
Sloths
Squirrels
Storks
Tasmanian Devil

Set 5

```
3  W  M  S  E  S  I  O  T  R  O  T  T  X  M
0  Q  M  A  R  S  U  P  I  A  L  S  S  S  V
D  B  G  Z  R  J  A  D  D  G  V  B  C  E  A
A  A  V  V  H  I  S  L  A  M  M  A  M  T  N
N  S  L  A  M  I  N  A  M  R  A  F  S  O  T
G  B  J  B  K  X  S  E  Y  O  X  R  M  Y  E
E  G  A  E  T  U  X  K  L  P  X  I  U  O  L
R  P  U  M  R  N  C  F  S  I  C  C  S  C  O
O  C  U  L  O  A  O  L  R  B  F  T  S  F  P
U  M  A  F  T  J  E  U  S  V  R  E  O  Y  E
S  W  V  T  F  S  I  R  B  A  E  I  P  A  S
A  C  L  M  A  I  U  U  M  D  P  J  O  A  A
N  E  X  E  I  M  N  P  A  N  T  H  E  R  S
I  M  W  G  E  M  H  S  I  T  I  H  B  D  G
M  X  T  L  P  I  Y  F  B  U  L  T  N  V  R
A  J  A  D  B  G  A  S  Q  R  E  B  C  A  L
L  T  D  I  Y  B  K  N  R  K  S  Q  W  R  B
S  P  A  P  V  O  S  O  J  E  S  W  F  K  D
U  N  V  B  N  O  D  L  G  Y  S  J  V  S  Y
S  J  G  O  R  I  L  L  A  S  A  S  A  E  H
```

Word List

30 Dangerous Animals
Aardvarks
Amphibians
Antelopes
Cattle
Coyotes
Farm Animals
Gorillas
Lemurs

Mammals
Marine Life
Marsupials
Opossums
Panthers
Puffins
Reptiles
Tortoises
Turkeys

Walrus
Weasels
Yaks

Set 1

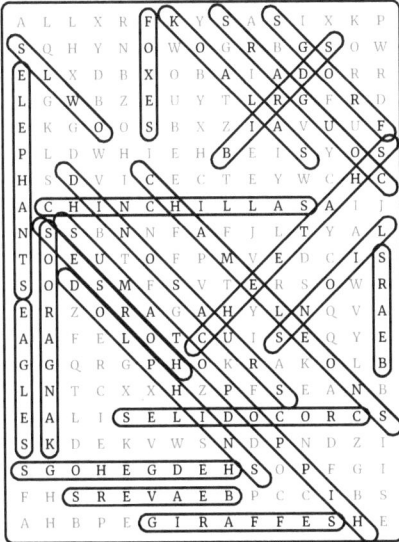

Set 2

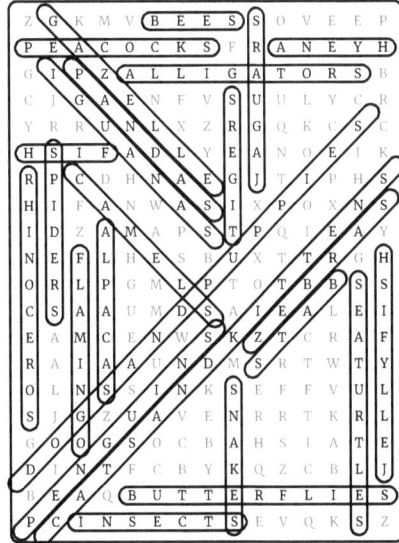

Set 3

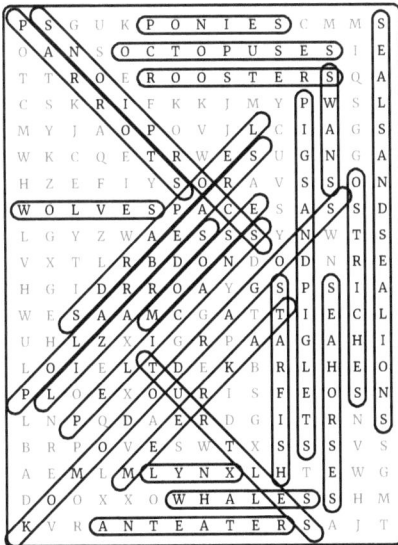

Set 4

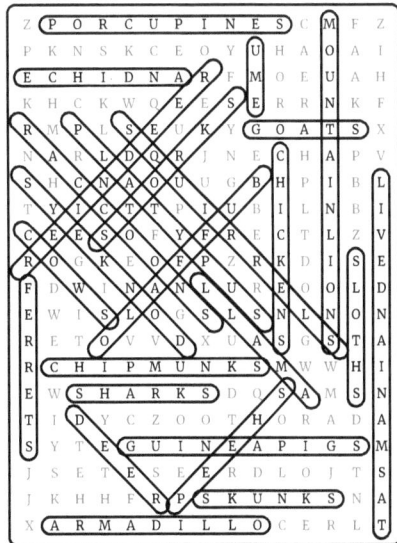

Set 5

```
3 W M S E S I O T R O T  T X M
0 Q M A R S U P I A L S  S E V
D B G Z R J A D D G V B  C T A
A V V H I S L A M M A M  E N
N S L A M I N A M R A F  S O T
B J B K X S E Y O X R M  Y E
G A E T U X K L P X I O  C L
R P U M R N C F S I C C  F O
O C U L O A L R B F R P
U M A F T J E U S V R E  A E
S W V T F S I R B A E I  A S
A C L M A I U M D P J O  A
N E X E I M N P A N T H  E R S
I M W G E H S I T I H B  D G
M X T L P I Y F B U L T  N R
A J A D B G A S Q R E B  C L
L T D I Y B K N R K S Q  W B
S A P V O S O J E S W F
U N V B N O D L G Y S J  V
S J G O R I L L A S A S  A E H
```

Puzzle 1

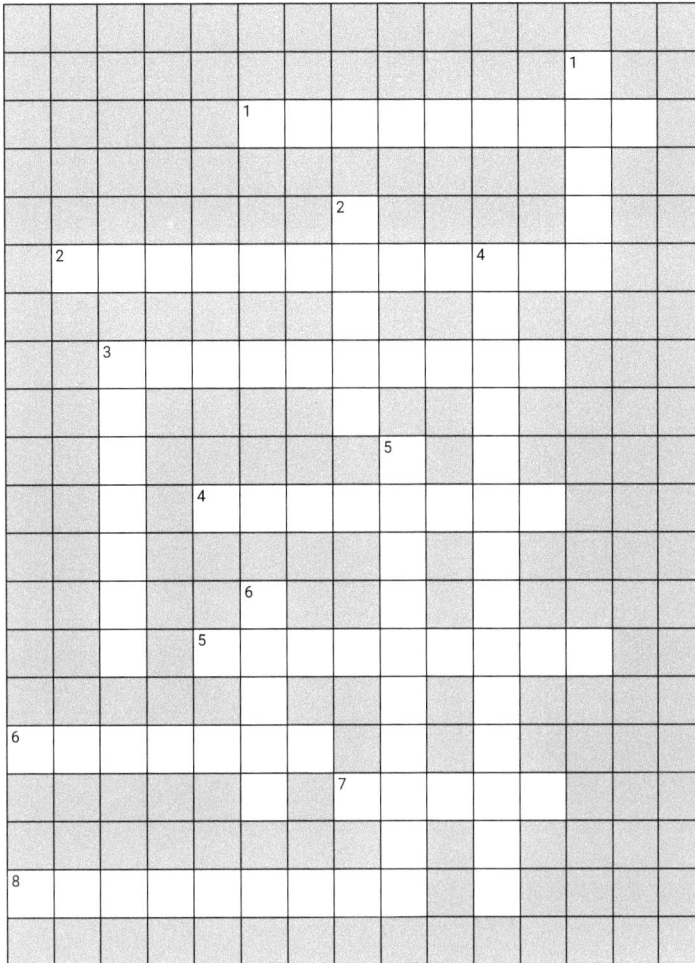

ACROSS
1. Dinosaurs
2. Caterpillars
3. Crocodiles
4. Dolphins
5. Hedgehogs
6. Beavers
7. Foxes
8. Elephants

DOWN
1. Frogs
2. Birds
3. Cougars
4. Apes and Monkeys
5. Chameleons
6. Bears

Puzzle 2

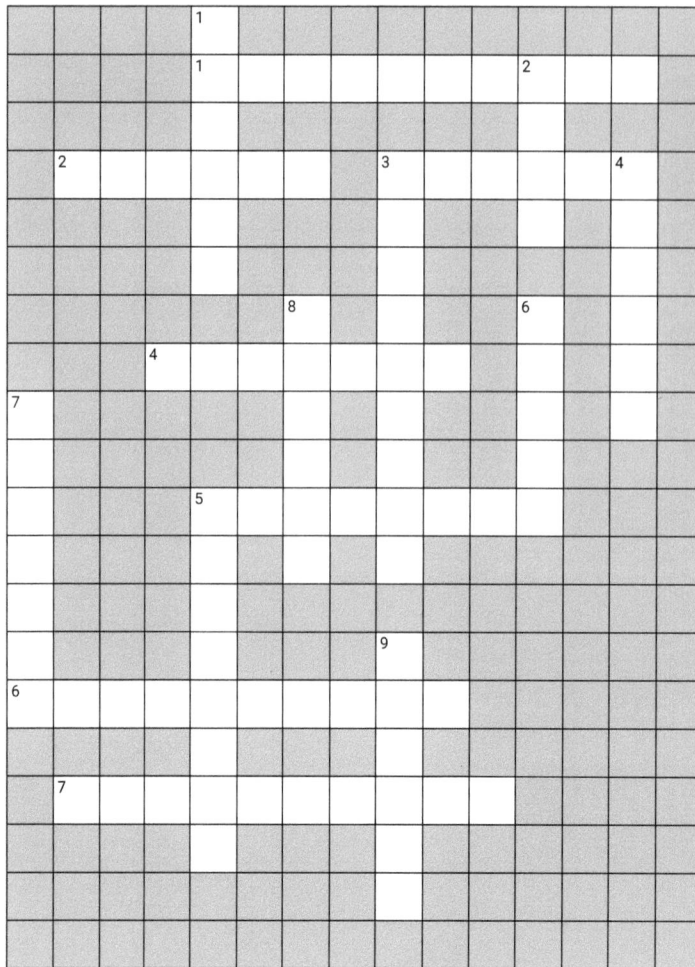

ACROSS
1. Alligators
2. Tigers
3. Koalas
4. Alpacas
5. Peacocks
6. Sea Turtles
7. Rhinoceros

DOWN
1. Camels
2. Owls
3. Kangaroos
4. Snakes
5. Penguins
6. Lions
7. Spiders
8. Pandas
9. Zebras

Puzzle 3

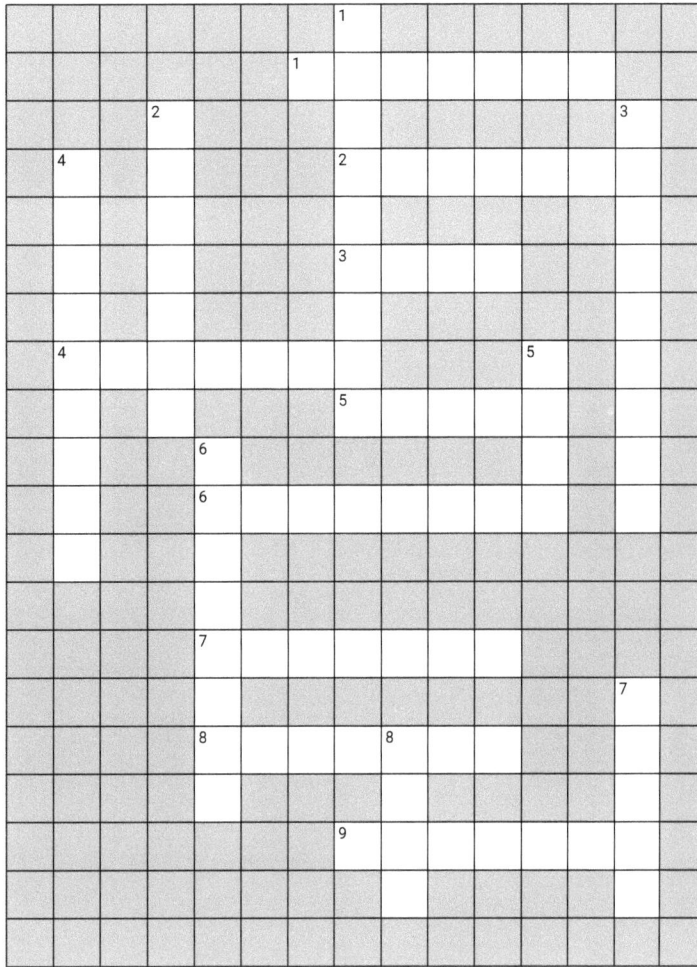

ACROSS
1. Meerkat
2. Lizards
3. Fish
4. Parrots
5. Hyena
6. Leopards
7. Iguanas
8. Gazelle
9. Insects

DOWN
1. Jellyfish
2. Jaguars
3. Ostriches
4. Octopuses
5. Bats
6. Flamingo
7. Moose
8. Lynx

Puzzle 4

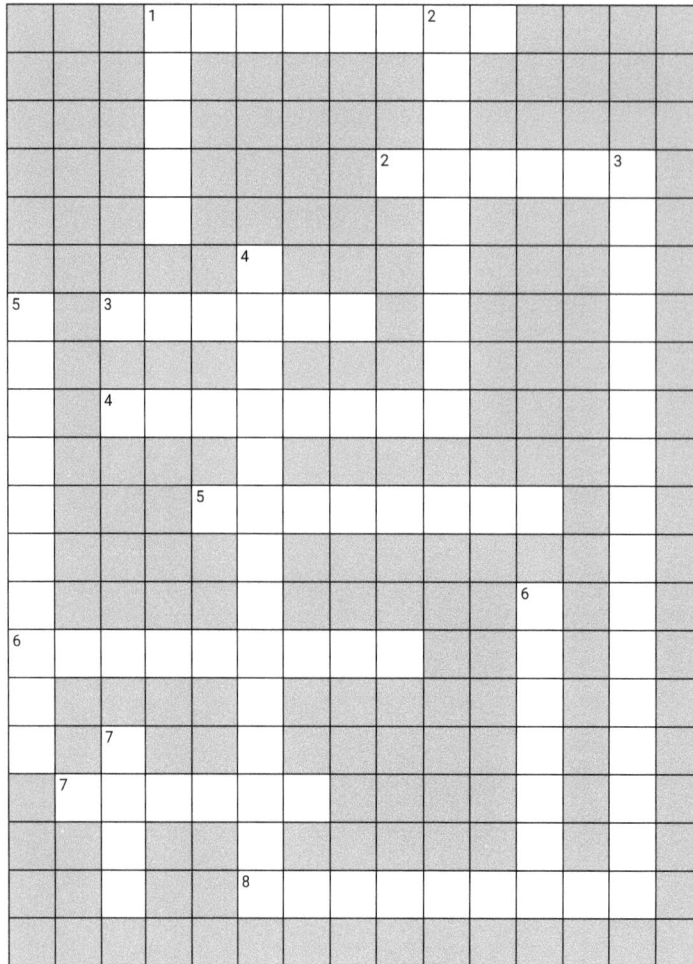

ACROSS
1. Starfish
2. Whales
3. Ponies
4. Roosters
5. Anteater
6. Armadillo
7. Wolves
8. Scorpions

DOWN
1. Swans
2. Seahorses
3. Seals and Sea Lions
4. Pigs and Piglets
5. Polar Bears
6. Buffalo
7. Cows

Puzzle 5

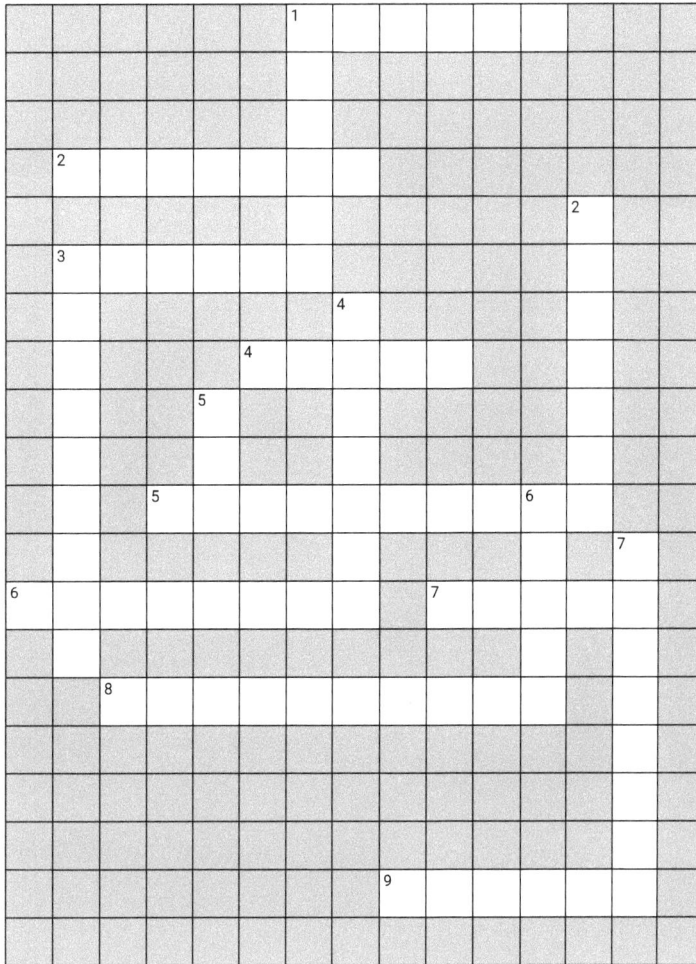

ACROSS
1. Sloths
2. Echidna
3. Storks
4. Sheep
5. Guinea Pigs
6. Platypus
7. Llama
8. Porcupines
9. Sharks

DOWN
1. Skunks
2. Donkeys
3. Squirrels
4. Ferrets
5. Emu
6. Goats
7. Raccoons

Puzzle 6

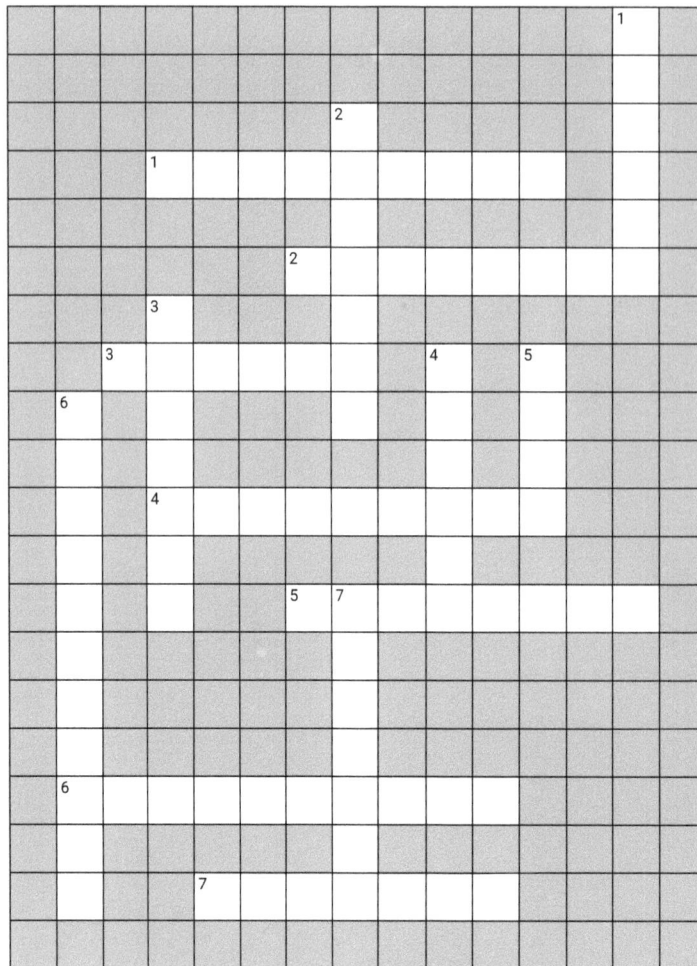

ACROSS
1. Tortoises
2. Gorillas
3. Cattle
4. Aardvarks
5. Opossums
6. Amphibians
7. Weasels

DOWN
1. Lemurs
2. Coyotes
3. Mammals
4. Walrus
5. Yaks
6. Farm Animals
7. Puffins

Puzzle 1

Puzzle 2

Puzzle 3

Puzzle 4

Puzzle 5

- SLOTHS
- SKUNK
- ECHIDNA
- DONKEY
- STORKS
- SQUIRREL
- FERRETS
- SHEEP
- EMU
- GUINEAPIG
- GOOSE
- PLATYPUS
- LLAMA
- RACCOON
- PORCUPINES
- SHARKS

Puzzle 6

- LEMURS
- CY
- TORTOISES
- GORILLAS
- MOTT
- CATTLE
- WALLABY
- YAK
- FAMINGOS / FLAMINGOS
- AARDVARKS
- OPOSSUMS
- AMPHIBIANS
- WEASELS

www.ingramcontent.com/pod-product-compliance
Lightning Source LLC
Chambersburg PA
CBHW060827270326
41931CB00002B/90